The Clever Teens' Guide to

The Russian Revolution

Felix Rhodes

The Clever Teens' series:

The Clever Teens' Guide to World War One

The Clever Teens' Guide to the Russian Revolution

The Clever Teens' Guide to Nazi Germany

The Clever Teens' Guide to World War Two

The Clever Teens' Guide to The Cold War

The Clever Teens' Tales from World War One

The Clever Teens' Tales from World War Two

Table of Contents

Visit **https://rupertcolley.com/category/soviet-union-russia/** for 13 articles expanding on topics covered here.

Nineteenth Century Russia

The communist system unleashed by the Russian Revolution of 1917 was the greatest political experiment ever conducted. The revolution promised freedom from the shackles of imperialism, corruption and exploitation but until its collapse in 1991, the peoples of the vast Soviet empire endured 70 years of misguided socialism and totalitarianism.

The last Russian tsar, Nicholas II, ruled over a vast empire that was backward, impoverished and largely resentful of his autocratic rule. Its people demanded reform and change. It was the outbreak of war in 1914 and the strain of war that finally, in March 1917, brought down the tsar and the 300-year-old Romanov dynasty.

But the Provisional Government that overthrew the tsar

proved equally ineffectual at addressing the needs of Russia's major problems. Only the representatives of the workers, or 'soviets', seemed to understand the problems that lay at the heart of the empire. And from the various parties of the Soviets emerged one party and, at its helm, one man that promised a new socialist utopia. It was to this party, the Bolshevik party, and this man, Vladimir Lenin, that Russia staked its future. The consequences shaped the entire Twentieth Century and its ramifications were felt across the world.

Alexander II

Between 1853 and 1856, Russia was embroiled in the Crimean War, fighting an alliance made up of Great Britain, France and Turkey. In March 1855, Alexander II succeeded his father as the tsar of Russia. Alexander, knowing his country was on the brink of total humiliation, helped bring the war to an end, signing the Treaty of Paris.

The war confirmed Russia's military inferiority, its weak infrastructure and, based on serfdom, its backward economy. Alexander knew if Russia was to survive, he needed to modernize his empire.

Alexander instigated a vast improvement in

communication, namely expanding Russia's rail network from just 660 miles of track (linking Moscow and St Petersburg) in the 1850s to over 14,000 miles within thirty years, which, in turn, aided Russia's industrial and economic expansion.

Alexander's reformist zeal restructured the judicial system which included the introduction of trial by jury. Military reform saw the introduction of conscription, the reduction of military service from 25 years to six, and the establishment of military schools.

Alexander II, 1870.

But reform only brought the demand for more. And so, on March 3, 1861, Alexander II issued what promised to be the most revolutionary reform in Russia's history – his *Manifesto on the Emancipation of the Serfs*. Russia's 25 million peasants had worked as virtual slaves for generations. Now, they were to be given ownership of 85 per cent of Russia's land, thus freeing them from their bondage to the wealthy landowners. Serfs were given the right to own property and set up their own businesses. Landowners tried to resist but, as they were told by the tsar, "It is better to abolish serfdom from above than to wait for the time when it will begin to abolish itself from below". In other words, the tsar didn't want a revolution on his hands.

The emancipation of the serfs was received enthusiastically until the full provisions of the 400-page act were known. The peasants had to buy the land from the nobles, usually at an inflated price. Very few could afford anything but the smallest of plots. So those unable to pay were given a loan by the government, repayable at six per cent over 49 years. Until payment was complete, the peasant would have to continue working for the landowner. The peasant, technically freed from serfdom, was no better off and no happier. Resentment was rife. This was land which the tsars had taken from the peasants in the first instance and given to the nobles thus the peasants resented having to buy back land they regarded as rightfully their own.

Alexander may have considered himself a reformist tsar but he firmly resisted all calls for any form of democracy – so there was to be no parliament or freedom of expression – it remained illegal to criticize the tsar or his government. He continued to rule by autocracy – where all means of power, without limit, are concentrated in the hands of one person. Anti-government groups formed and met in secret, many prepared to use violence to achieve their aims.

Over the years, Alexander survived a number of assassination attempts. But on March 13, 1881, the tsar was not so lucky. A group of anarchists called the People's Will threw a bomb at Alexander's carriage as it drove through the streets of Russia's capital, St Petersburg, killing the tsar. (Until 1924, St Petersburg was the capital of Russia).

Alexander III

Hours before his death, Alexander II had reluctantly signed a raft of proposals for constitutional reforms that included the establishment of a parliament, a Duma, the first step towards a constitutional monarchy. The terrorists (all of whom were hanged) had unwittingly aborted any chance of constitutional reform. Instead, Alexander's son, Alexander III, immediately withdrew the proposals, undid many of his father's reforms and intensified the level of repression.

Alexander III rejected his father's liberalism and his belief in reform which, he believed, weakened the monarchy. Democracy was the "biggest lie of our time", and, as he wrote, "the very idea of electoral government is something I will never accept". Russia needed to become one nation with one identity and one language hence ethnic traditions and languages were severely repressed. Russia's secret police, which his father had downsized, was enlarged and anyone suspected of revolutionary sympathy was exiled to Siberia.

In St Petersburg in March 1887, members of the People's Will were arrested and found guilty of planning to assassinate Alexander III. Most of them were executed, including a 21-year-old called Alexander Ulyanov. His execution shocked and radicalised his younger, 17-year-old brother, Vladimir, who, himself, became a fervent radical, determined to bring about a proletariat uprising and to take power away from the Romanovs and their privileged elites. He read the works of revolutionary intellectuals, becoming devoted to the works of Karl Marx, joined activist groups, spoke passionately about the need for revolution, and changed his name.

His new name was Vladimir Lenin.

Nicholas II

On November 1, 1894, aged only 49, Alexander III died of kidney disease. The throne passed to his 26-year-old son, Nicholas.

Nicholas II followed in his father's autocratic footsteps. When a delegation of peasant representatives came to petition him to allow a small measure of autonomy, Nicholas dismissed them out of hand: "I am determined, for the good of the nation, to uphold the principle of absolute autocracy, as firmly and as resolutely as my late lamented father".

Nicholas II, 1898.

But while his father had been a physically strong and authoritarian man, Nicholas was weak, nervous and prone to agree with whoever spoke to him last. Aware of his own weakness, he once described himself as "without will and without character".

In 1898, a new revolutionary socialist party was formed, the Russian Social Democratic Labour Party (RSDLP). Three years later came the Socialist Revolutionary Party (SR). Neither party shied away from the use of violence to further their aims, but agreement on how those objectives should be reached differed.

In 1902, Vladimir Lenin joined the ranks of the RSDLP, and, the same year, published a political pamphlet called *What Is To Be Done?* In it, Lenin argued that left to their own devices, Russia's working class would remain politically lethargic; it was up to dedicated revolutionaries, such as himself, to educate the working classes about the writings of Marx and steer the Marxist revolution on their behalf. Karl Marx believed in a socialist revolution, in which the working classes would overthrow the capitalists and seize power for the good of all.

The RSDLP, banned in Russia, held its second congress in London. Lenin expanded on his ideas, arguing that the party needed to remain small but professional and that they, as Marxists, had to become the "vanguard of the proletariat".

Opposing him were those who firmly believed that the party needed to expand its numbers. The opposing views were so fixed that it split the party – those supporting Lenin breaking away to become known as the Bolsheviks (meaning the "majority", even though they were in the minority) and those remaining the Mensheviks (meaning the "minority").

Russo-Japanese War

On February 8, 1904, a Japanese fleet launched a surprise attack on the Russian naval squadron at Port Arthur in southern Manchuria in China. The Japanese government had been incensed by what they saw as Russia's presence just 600 miles from Japan. The year before, Russia had reneged on an agreement to withdraw its troops from Manchuria, so Japan decided to attack. On May 27, 1905, the Japanese and Russian fleets engaged in a battle in the Tsushima Straits, a stretch of sea between Korea and Japan. Russia's navy suffered severely, losing eight battleships and seven cruisers, and its defeat caused shockwaves at home.

Nicholas II had hoped the Russo-Japanese War would deflect attention from domestic issues and raise his popularity. When advised to seek peace, Nicholas II refused. He didn't for one moment think Russia would lose. But with the war going against Russia, Nicholas had no choice but to sue for peace. Russia's defeat, and the loss of some 120,000 Russian soldiers and sailors against a supposedly inferior foe, dented Russia's reputation as a world power. Instead of defusing internal problems, it merely intensified them leading to what became known as the Russian Revolution of 1905.

1905

On Sunday January 22, 1905, 200,000 workers from St Petersburg, led by an Orthodox priest, Father Georgi Gapon, marched towards the Winter Palace armed with a petition to be presented to the tsar demanding widespread political reform.

Although trade unions were banned, Father Gapon had been allowed to set up a workers' assembly in 1904 under the supervision of the tsar's secret police, the Okhrana, with whom he had ties. In early January 1905, after four workers were sacked from their jobs at the huge Putilov Plant in St Petersburg, Gapon called his workers out on strike. The strike spread and culminated with the march on the Winter Palace and the delivery of the petition.

Penned by Father Gapon, the petition, signed by a staggering 135,000 people, demanded the right to strike; a reduction in the working day from 11 to eight hours; the introduction of universal suffrage; and an end to Russia's on-going war with Japan.

Gapon and the demonstrators believed that essentially, Nicholas II, whom they affectionately called their "little father", was a good man who had their best interests at heart and that once he knew the extent of the workers' discontent, he would put in place the means to address their grievances. The march was good-natured with women and children leading the way, bearing religious icons and portraits of the tsar and singing patriotic songs.

10,000 armed troops were told to expect trouble. Blocking the demonstrators' route to the palace, the troops fired directly into the crowds. Up to 200 civilians were killed and many more wounded. One eyewitness described the "pools of blood on the white snow, the whips, the whooping of the gendarmes, the dead, the injured, the children shot".

Despite his faith in autocracy, Tsar Nicholas II had been generally well liked and respected by his people. "Bloody Sunday", as the massacre became known, changed everything.

Tsarist troops firing on civilians, St Petersburg, January 22, 1905.

More disaster for the tsar followed just five months later. Morale in the Russian navy was low. On June 27, 1905, sailors on board the battleship *Potemkin*, moored off the Ukrainian coast, refused to eat their soup which, they found, contained maggots. The crew mutinied, killing the captain and several other officers. The crew, taking control of the ship, sailed it under the red flag of revolution to Odessa in Ukraine where they hoped to receive support from striking workers. But, unable to land and fearing they might be attacked by ships still loyal to the Russian fleet, the mutineers decided to head for Romania, where they surrendered to the local authorities.

"Bloody Sunday" and the Potemkin mutiny were far from isolated incidents. The tsar's authority teetered as the whole nation fell into a state of violence, anarchy and revolution. His prime minister, Sergei Witte, knew things had to change and managed to persuade Nicholas into establishing a parliament, the "Duma". Although describing it as a "terrible decision", Nicholas finally relented and on October 17, 1905, issued the "October Manifesto". The manifesto, composed by Witte, promised a degree of civil rights, including "freedom of conscience, speech, assembly and association", and the elected parliament. It was, on paper at least, a huge step forward – after 300 years of autocracy, the tsar was offering parliamentary democracy. But for many in Russia it was a case of "too little, too late". The damage had been done; Nicholas was too unpopular. Many criticized the October Manifesto as "nothing more than a scrap of paper", and that the tsar had acted not because he wanted to but because events had forced it upon him. They were right; in signing the Manifesto, Nicholas felt "sick with shame at this betrayal of the dynasty". The tsar firmly believed he had been appointed God's representative and saw no reason to dilute his divinely sanctioned rule. And the franchise was far from all-embracing – limited to the rich and educated. But the tsar had done enough – he'd kept the army on his side and his notional move towards democracy brought an end to revolution. At least for a while.

On the same day as Nicholas issued his manifesto, the first council of workers, or "Soviet", was established in St Petersburg. Soon, several cities, including Moscow, had their own soviets. They didn't last long. In December 1905, the tsar's police moved in and arrested the leaders. Lenin, who managed to evade arrest, fled to Zurich. He was not to step foot on Russian soil again for another twelve years.

1906 – 1913

Russia held its first elections during the spring of 1906 – albeit with a limited franchise. A party called the Kadets, led by Pavel Milyukov, won most seats but immediately their power was reigned in when the tsar introduced a new constitution which effectively restricted the powers of the Duma and allowed Nicholas to veto its laws and maintain his autocracy. The tsar seemed to have forgotten why it had been necessary to introduce his manifesto in the first place. Ministers, appointed by the tsar, would report to him, not the Duma, and he was in sole charge of both foreign affairs and the military and, in cases of emergency, the tsar could by-pass the Duma entirely. This first Duma, much to Nicholas's horror, demanded too much reform so after two months, he had it dissolved. The same day, July 21, he appointed Pyotr Stolypin his new prime minister.

Stolypin's two main objectives as prime minister were to win the peasantry over and, at the same time, suppress the radicals. He knew the task would be a difficult one: "In no country is the public more anti-governmental than in Russia," he once told a colleague.

Stolypin wanted to encourage the peasantry to set up as independent farmers, helped by government loans. He believed that if he made the peasants' lives more content and their lot more prosperous, it would end political instability in the countryside and, as a result, the peasants would show greater loyalty, not to the Duma, but to the tsar and his autocratic rule.

Pyotr Stolypin.

In the towns, industrial growth continued apace but the welfare of the workers came well below the interests of the owners on the list of government priorities. Working 12 to 14-hour days, they lived in squalor, their wages fell, and they were prohibited from forming unions.

Reform went hand-in-hand with repression – up to 3,000 revolutionaries or suspected revolutionaries were executed between 1906 and 1911, victim to the hangman's noose or, as it became known, "Stolypin's necktie", while the "Stolypin wagon" exiled vast numbers of political opponents to Siberia. Newspapers unsympathetic to the tsar were closed down.

The second Duma, instituted March 1907, blocked Stolypin's reforms but the prime minister was not to be denied. With the tsar's backing, he managed to have the Duma dissolved within three months. Having changed the voting system, thereby ensuring a reduced peasant voice and a greater return of conservative and moderate members, Stolypin managed to form a third Duma, November 1907; one that was pro-tsarist. And this one lasted a whole five years.

But Stolypin's reforms may have been too ambitious for the tsar's liking and persistent rumours hinted that the prime minister was about to be dismissed. On September 14, 1911, Stolypin, who refused to wear a bullet-proof vest on account of its foul smell, was attending the opera in Kiev with the tsar and his two eldest daughters when he was shot. He fell, crying, "I am happy to die for my tsar", and, unbuttoning his jacket, blessed Nicholas with a sign of the cross.

Many believed that the assassination had been officially sanctioned. Why, for example, did Nicholas's secret police, the Okhrana, allow the assassin, 24-year-old Dmitry Bogrov, access to the opera house when they apparently knew he was carrying a revolver?

Full of remorse, Nicholas kneeled at Stolypin's hospital bed, begging his forgiveness. The prime minister, aged 49, died on September 18. Nicholas immediately halted the investigation into the killing, and Bogrov, who, it turned out, was an agent of the Okhrana, was hastily hanged before being properly interviewed.

With Pyotr Stolypin's assassination, Russia's programme of reform came to an abrupt end.

The tsar now effectively ignored the workings of the Duma; the lofty ideals of the 1905 October Manifesto had been quietly forgotten and the status quo of Russia's autocracy re-established.

Tsar Nicholas II and his wife, Alexandra, had five children – four girls and a boy, Alexei, the youngest, born 1904, the tsarevich or heir to the throne. Alexei was cursed with haemophilia and nothing the doctors prescribed had any effect. But there was one man capable of treating Alexei's affliction – the strange mystic, Grigori Rasputin. Rasputin had arrived in St Petersburg in 1903, his reputation as a holy man preceding him. Summoned by the Royal Family, Rasputin was able to stem the bleeding of the tsar's youngest child. Only Rasputin, it seemed, could treat the poor boy. Thus, he formed a bond with the royal couple and enjoyed their support. But the people didn't like Rasputin and resented his influence on the royal family.

War

On June 28, 1914, a Bosnian-Serb named Gavrilo Princip assassinated the heir to the Austro-Hungarian throne. Austria-Hungary had been troubled by Serbia for a while and the assassination provided them with the excuse to exert their authority over their neighbour. With the backing of their powerful ally, Germany, the Austro-Hungarian government presented Serbia with an ultimatum designed to be so humiliating to Serbian national pride that it would be rejected. It was. But Serbia, in turn, appealed to its own powerful ally, Russia. War seemed inevitable.

On July 30, Russia began to mobilize. The following day, the German government sent Russia an ultimatum, demanding it to cease mobilization within twelve hours. Russia did not, hence on August 1, Germany declared war on Russia.

Germany declared war on France, Russia's ally, on August 3, and the following day, Britain declared war on Germany. The First World War had started.

The war was briefly popular in Russia – the motherland needed defending and domestic issues were, for a short while, forgotten. St Petersburg was given a new, less Germanic-sounding name, Petrograd. People came out on the streets to cheer the tsar and back the crusade to save Russia. Even Lenin was not opposed to the war – but for very different reasons. Lenin hoped that war would lead, ultimately, to civil war against the tsar and his bourgeois government and usher in a new socialist order. He saw it in terms of a capitalist war, a "slaughter of the proletariat of all lands by setting the hired slaves of one nation against the hired slaves of another".

By the end of 1914, Russia had suffered one defeat after another. 1.8 million Russian troops had already been killed in a war that was still less than six months old. The war wasn't so popular now.

By mid-1915, the Duma was demanding greater powers with which to deal with the on-going catastrophe. The tsar, as always, refused and promptly suspended the Duma. Nicholas appointed himself commander of his country's military (a disastrous decision because as things went wrong, he was held accountable). With the tsar away from Petrograd, Tsarina

Alexandra made many of the domestic decisions in her husband's absence. Being a German, she was generally disliked by the Russian populace who questioned where her loyalties lay. The fact she still retained her devotion to Rasputin certainly didn't help matters. She appointed and sacked a rapid succession of ministers and prime ministers under, it was suspected, Rasputin's mercurial influence.

Grigori Rasputin, 1916.

On December 29, 1916, Rasputin, lured to the Petrograd palace of Prince Felix Yusupov, was poisoned, shot and clubbed and finally drowned in the River Neva. In killing Rasputin, the Prince and his accomplices believed they were acting in the best interests of the nation and the monarchy. However, more recent evidence points increasingly to the involvement of the British who were alarmed by reports that Rasputin was trying to persuade the tsarina to use her influence to remove Russian troops from the war. The consequences of this would have allowed Germany to transfer 350,000 troops and equipment from the Eastern Front to the Western Front, greatly bolstering its forces against the Allies – an alarming prospect for the British and the French. Thus it is now believed to have been a British spy, Oswald Rayner (who had met Yusupov at Oxford), who dealt Rasputin the fatal blow.

The February Revolution

The removal of Rasputin however did not save the monarchy. Proletariat resentment in Russia showed no signs of abating. Desertion from Russia's military was rife; the economy was in chaos, food was desperately short and life for the average Russian was miserable. On March 8, 1917, (International Women's Day), thousands of women in Petrograd protested over the lack of bread. Very soon they were joined by factory workers from across the city. The strikers and protestors demanded bread, they demanded freedom, and they demanded an end to the war. The tsar, 500 miles away in the Belarus town of Moghilev and refusing to leave the front and underestimating the extent or seriousness of the unrest, ordered in the troops. Petrograd-based troops fired and massacred scores of protestors. They were joined by soldiers sent from the front to reinforce the Petrograd garrisons, but these troops refused to shoot unarmed civilians, and instead joined their ranks.

Demonstrators on the streets of Petrograd, March 1917.

The protest spread. Soon, people in towns and cities across the Russian empire were in open revolt. Soviets, which had been violently squashed at the end of 1905, suddenly reappeared. Members and former members of the Duma together with the Petrograd Soviet formed a new government, a provisional one.

Members of the new provisional government went to see the tsar. They met in a train outside a town called Pskov, about 190 miles south of Petrograd. They told him in no uncertain terms that his situation was unsustainable – he had no choice but to abdicate. He hesitated but ultimately knew he had no choice.

After 603 years, the Romanov dynasty was at an end.

The new provisional government announced its commitment to the war, much to the relief of their Western Allies, Great Britain and France. Russia's soldiers however were not so keen. Desertion reached epidemic proportions – 30,000 soldiers a day by the end of May 1917.

Dual Power

Between them, the Petrograd Soviet and the provisional government ruled together, the "Dual Power". The Provisional Government was "provisional" in that they fully intended to hold free national elections. They released political prisoners from the jails, disbanded the tsar's dreaded secret police force and abolished the death penalty. The Provisional Government may have possessed the formal authority and introduced their much-welcomed reforms but it was the Soviet that controlled the real levers of power, including, crucially, the loyalty of the army, and offered only conditional support to the government. Indeed, the Petrograd Soviet issued its first order, "Order No.1", that its members should only obey the

Provisional Government if the Soviet agreed with it. The Soviet, at this stage, was dominated by the Mensheviks, Kadets and Socialist Revolutionaries (SRs). The Bolsheviks were notable only by their absence. Vladimir Lenin, Bolshevik leader, had missed the February Revolution, still in exile in Switzerland.

Lenin had no way of getting back to Russia through German-held territory. Yet, it was the Germans who supplied the solution for Lenin. They wanted Russia out of the war so that they could concentrate all their efforts on defeating the British and the French on the Western Front. Knowing Lenin's presence in Russia would be akin to a Bolshevik virus, capable of destroying the pro-war provisional government, they secreted Lenin back into Russia on a sealed train.

Arriving back in Petrograd in early April, Lenin made a triumphal speech: "The Russian revolution accomplished by you has prepared the way and opened a new epoch. The worldwide socialist revolution is dawning; European capitalism is on the brink of collapse. Long live the worldwide socialist revolution!" The February Revolution and the overthrow of the tsar were, for Lenin, mere preludes to the full, proletariat, socialist revolution, the "new epoch", that was just around the corner.

Vladimir Lenin, c1918.

Lenin argued with the Mensheviks over the direction of the revolution. The Mensheviks urged caution, suggesting that the working classes were not yet ready for power. Lenin disagreed. He wanted power and he wanted it immediately. On his return to Petrograd, he produced a ten-point manifesto that became known as his "April Theses". In it, he condemned the "bourgeois" Provisional Government and condemned all those, ie the Mensheviks and the SRs, who openly or quietly supported it. He finished off by introducing the slogan, "All power to the soviets!" He would have preferred the rallying cry of "All power to the Bolsheviks", but he knew the

Bolshevik presence and influence within the soviet was, for the time being, limited.

Meanwhile, the provisional government confirmed its commitment to the war. They were, said Lenin, no different to the tsarist regime.

On June 16, the Soviet held its first "Congress of Russian Soviets". Proceedings were dominated by the leading soviet parties; the Bolsheviks were still a minority despite Lenin's commanding presence. The congress argued again over whether the time was ripe for a socialist revolution. The Mensheviks and the SRs held onto their position that the time was not ripe, that for the sake of the long-term, the soviet had to maintain its uneasy alliance with the provisional government. The Menshevik leader argued that "At the present, there is no party in Russia that can say: give us power, we are ready to take it. There is no such party". To which Lenin famously replied, "There is such a party!"

In July, Prince Georgy Lvov resigned as head of the provisional government to be replaced by his minister of war, Alexander Kerensky. The government had not managed to fix the economy and food remained in short supply. Kerensky was also committed to the on-going war and hoped Russian success on the battlefield would encourage his countrymen to continue the fight.

On July 1, Kerensky launched a new offensive against Austro-Hungarian and German forces in Galicia. Led by Kerensky's talented general, Lavr Kornilov, the "Kerensky Offensive", as it became known, started well for the Russians, defeating the Austro-Hungarians. The Germans proved a harder nut to crack. Russian casualties soared as the Germans counterattacked, forcing the Russian army into a hasty retreat. Soldiers deserted and fled for home; officers who tried in vain to get their men to hold their ground were shot.

July Days

Back in Petrograd, workers and soldiers took to the streets brandishing Lenin's slogan, "All power to the Soviets!" From July 16–20, with Kerensky's offensive proving to be such a catastrophe, half a million workers and soldiers rebelled, demanding an immediate end to the war in what became known as the "July Days" demonstration.

Initially, the Bolsheviks gave the demonstrations their backing but soon became anxious, fearing that the soviets were not quite ready for full power after all. Too late. Troops loyal to the Provisional Government appeared to restore order by force and arrest the Bolshevik leadership.

Lenin, who had distanced himself from the demonstrators, went into hiding. Disguised as a haymaker, he hid away for a month in a straw hut ("Lenin's Hut") in the forests next to Lake Razliv, north of Petrograd. At the end of August, Lenin left Razliv for Finland. Disguised by a clean-shave and a wig, he travelled under the name of K. Ivanov, a worker from an arms factory. Other leading Bolsheviks, including Leon Trotsky, still caught in Petrograd, were arrested and imprisoned.

Troops of the Provisional Government open fire on demonstrators during the July Day riots, July 1917.

The "July Days" demonstrations may have been easily crushed, but it caused serious disturbances within the provisional government. Members of the Kadets deserted the government, resulting in a new coalition comprising or temporary alliance composed mostly of Mensheviks and Socialist Revolutionaries. Kerensky was elated – he had brought the moderate socialists into his government and, in dealing with the July demonstrators, had dealt with the Bolsheviks.

But the Bolsheviks were not yet finished. Under the slogan of "Peace, bread and land", they were able to exploit the groundswell of popular unrest and disillusionment. The government had gunned down workers on the streets, they cried, they were no better than the tsarists. Workers, peasants and former soldiers established bands of militia, called Red Guards or "revolutionary armies".

While the Soviets armed themselves, Kerensky and his new coalition government found itself facing a new threat – on September 1, German forces took the Latvian city of Riga – the enemy was now within 300 miles of Petrograd. The situation for the government, both at home and on the battlefield, was perilous.

By mid-September, the Bolsheviks had become the dominant force within the Soviets across the country, including, most importantly, in both Petrograd and Moscow. Lenin, still detained in Finland, pressed his party to overthrow

Kerensky's government but the Bolsheviks in Petrograd, led by Lev Kamenev and Grigory Zinoviev, advised restraint.

Lavr Kornilov, 1917.

Kerensky's general, Lavr Kornilov, taking matters into his own hands, decided to destroy the Petrograd soviet for once and for all. In August, Kornilov and his troops advanced on the capital. At first, Kerensky welcomed this development, wishing to see an end to the Bolsheviks. But then he got word that Kornilov planned to overthrow the government as well. Now in a state of panic, Kerensky turned to the Petrograd soviet for help. He offered the Bolsheviks a deal – he would release all those locked-up following the "July Days" demonstrations and he would lend the Bolsheviks large stacks of armoury and weapons with which to fight off Kornilov and his men. The deal was struck.

The Bolsheviks gathered their arms and support. Workers sympathetic to the Bolshevik cause controlled all the major rail links into the capital and were able to sabotage Kornilov's advance into the city. Kornilov's attempt to seize power floundered before it had had chance to start. Kerensky's relief was short-lived – he'd given the Bolsheviks greater legitimacy, provided them with huge amounts of armoury, which they now refused to return, and had crucially undermined his authority both within his military and with the Russian people. But Kerensky was still confident he could contain the Bolshevik menace, convinced that if it came, he'd be able to "crush" any Bolshevik uprising.

Lenin knew differently.

But with Lenin still in Finland, it fell to Leon Trotsky to rally the troops. With Kerensky's weapons, he organised the Bolshevik "Red Guard". All that was needed now was the return of Lenin himself. And on October 23, the man duly returned – disguised as a railway worker. At a meeting of the Party Central Committee in Petrograd that evening, the party voted ten to two that "an armed uprising is inevitable, and that the time for it is fully ripe". Again Lev Kamenev and Grigory Zinoviev urged caution. Lenin refused to listen. The days for caution were over.

The October Revolution

The Bolsheviks, with Trotsky leading from the front, were ready to take the government's seat of power, the Winter Palace. Crowds gathered. At 21:45 on November 7, sailors on board the *Aurora*, anchored on the banks of the River Neva, fired a number of blank shots at the palace. Ministers inside the palace, understandably believing they were under attack, panicked. At 2 am on November 8, revolutionary troops stormed the palace, perhaps hoping for a heroic and symbolic fight – in the event they found the place defended by a few bored teenaged guards and women. Most of them were happy to side with the revolutionaries. Hence, the Winter Palace fell without bloodshed. It wasn't the glorious fight they'd hoped for. As Trotsky said, "The final act of revolution seems, after all this, too brief, too business-like". Kerensky, having lost the support of the military, had no one to turn to. He fled. The remaining ministers were arrested on the spot.

And thus, the Bolsheviks had gained power.

Leon Trotsky, c1921.

Later on the 8th, Lenin spoke triumphantly at the Second Congress of All-Russian Soviets in Petrograd and received a standing ovation. Power had passed into the hands of the Soviet, and the "Russian Soviet Federative Socialist Republic" was formally announced: "We shall now proceed to the construction of the socialist order".

The congress accepted Lenin's decrees on peace, thus bringing Russia's participation in the Great War to an end. Lenin announced his plans to redistribute the land to the peasants: land was declared state property and transferred over to peasants without compensation to the previous owners. The congress announced its intention to nationalise the nation's banks, church property and to hand the control of the factories to the workers. Lenin also announced a cabinet composed solely of Bolsheviks, the Council of People's Commissars. This caused a huge argument. The SRs and Mensheviks finally realised the lie behind Lenin's slogan. "All power to the Soviet". Lenin had no intention and never had any intention of sharing power with the soviets – only the Bolsheviks. In protest, they stormed out while Trotsky yelled at them – "You pitiful individuals! You are bankrupts. Your role is played out. Go where you belong – into the dustbin of history!"

A month later, as Lenin consolidated the Bolshevik hold on power, he founded the new secret police – the All-Russian Emergency Commission for Combating Counter-Revolution and Sabotage, or, to use its nickname, the "Cheka", with Felix Dzerzhinsky (Iron Felix) its head. The Cheka set to work – arresting anyone suspected of being a "counterrevolutionary" or "enemy of the people".

The now-defunct provisional government had been provisional in that it always intended to stage an election to elect a parliament and draw up a constitution. It failed to deliver. Lenin also promised an election – based on universal suffrage. He made good on his promise and on November 25, 1917, Russia went to the polls, the first free election in Russian history. Lenin anticipated victory and a mandate to rule. He was to be disappointed. The Socialist Revolutionaries won convincingly; the Bolsheviks came a poor second. The Mensheviks and the Kadets came third and fourth respectively. The result was a disaster for Lenin. Nevertheless, the Constituent Assembly convened in Petrograd's Tauride Palace on January 18, 1918.

Lenin was in a bad mood. The SRs may have won the election but his Bolsheviks still dominated the cabinet: "To relinquish the sovereign power of the Soviets for the sake of the bourgeois parliamentary system would now be a step backwards and would cause the collapse of the October workers' and peasants' revolution".

The Bolsheviks then marched out of the meeting leaving the rest of the assembly to argue amongst itself all through the night until the following morning when the palace's janitors forcibly removed them.

When, later that day, January 19, members of the assembly returned to Tauride Palace, they found the place locked and surrounded by Bolshevik soldiers. Russia's democratically elected assembly had lasted a mere 12 hours.

Lenin now tightened his grip on power. In 1918, he issued a constitution that, recognising the dictatorship of the proletariat, promised the "abolition of the exploitation of men by men, the abolition of the division of the people into classes, the suppression of exploiters, and the establishment of a socialist society".

Rival political parties were banned, Moscow became the new Russian capital, the calendar was changed, independent newspapers dissolved, a new greeting ("comrade") introduced, and the Red Army established. The Cheka was kept busy – executing enemies and perceived enemies and carting thousands off to Siberian camps, known as "gulags".

The End of Russia's War

The October Revolution effectively ended Russia's participation in the Great War. On December 16, 1917 Russia signed an armistice with Germany and its allies. But the formal treaty of surrender had still to be signed. Lenin ordered Trotsky to deal with it. The terms of the treaty, as dictated by the

Germans, were extremely harsh on Russia. Russia was to lose the Baltic States to Germany, the territories of Poland, Finland and a large part of Ukraine, almost a third of the Russian Empire's population, a third of its agricultural space and 90 per cent of its coal mines.

There were those within the party who thought Germany's demands were too much. But for Lenin, signing the treaty was a price worth paying for the sake of peace. They had no choice: Germany's "knees are on our chest", he declared. Thus, on March 3, 1918, under Lenin's orders, Trotsky signed the Treaty of Brest-Litovsk.

With Russia now out of the war, Germany was able to transfer huge numbers of men and equipment from its Eastern Front to fight Great Britain, France and their allies on the Western Front.

Five days later, on March 8, the Bolshevik party officially changed its name to the Russian Communist Party and Lenin moved the seat of the government from Petrograd to Russia's new capital, Moscow.

Execution of the Tsar

Following the tsar's abdication, the royal family had been kept under house arrest in various secret locations. In April 1918, they were transferred to Yekaterinburg in the Urals and kept in a former merchant's house.

The British government had wanted to offer Nicholas and his family asylum but King George V, Nicholas's cousin, refused, fearing that the presence of the fallen tsar in Britain could cause trouble.

Nicholas II and family, 1913.

The Bolsheviks feared that one day the Romanovs might be rescued and become a rallying point for their enemies. So they decided to act. Soon after midnight on July 17, 1918, the family was awakened, told to get dressed and washed, and taken down to the basement of the house.

The former royal couple sat down, with the 13-year-old Alexei sitting on his father's lap (both wore soldiers' shirts and caps) and the girls gathered behind their mother. Also with them, the family doctor and three servants who had remained loyal to the last.

Yakov Yurovsky, in charge of the house, led in a squad of executioners and read a short statement announcing the order for execution. An incredulous Nicholas said, "What?" before being shot dead by Yurovsky. The squad opened fire. But Alexandra and her daughters had, over the weeks, sewn their jewellery into their undergarments (in case they could be used for bartering at some point) and so to a degree were protected from the bullets. But they were finished off by bayonet and finally a shot each to the head.

Initially dumped down a mineshaft, the bodies were hastily buried in nearby forests. Their exact location remained a mystery until their discovery in 1979, although it would be a further 19 years before DNA confirmed their identification.

Civil War

The Bolshevik signing of the Treaty of Brest-Litovsk was too much for those already opposed to Lenin and his harsh rule. Anti-Bolshevik groups made up of SRs, Kadets and Mensheviks, together with different ethnic groups and nationalities and anyone simply opposed to the Bolsheviks, formed a loose alliance known as the Whites. They included a large number of monarchists (supporters of the deposed tsar) who, beyond a shared hatred of the Bolsheviks, had nothing in common with their new-found allies. The Russian Civil War was, at its most basic, a fight between the Reds and Whites. The Western Allies, determined to see Bolshevism finished, aided the Whites. Plus, they hoped the victorious Whites would resume fighting against the Germans on the Eastern Front and ease the pressure on the Western Front. Troops from Britain, France and the US fought alongside the Whites.

The civil war started badly for the Bolsheviks; their grip on power looked weaker by the month. They still had control of Moscow and Petrograd but elsewhere the Whites were supreme, edging nearer to the capital and former capital. Trotsky, a formidable organiser, galvanised the "Red Army", the "Reds".

Lenin making a speech to Red Army troops, 1919.

With the civil war raging, Lenin introduced an economic policy that he felt was necessary in order to win the civil war – "War Communism". The policy banned private enterprise, nationalised all industry, introduced strict rationing, confiscated agricultural surpluses in order to feed the cities and the Red Army, and forbade all strike action. Those who resisted were shot; richer peasants feared for their lives; hiding of grain was punishable by death. Freedom of expression was severely suppressed. The measures were deeply unpopular – but necessary, as far as Lenin was concerned, to win the war.

On August 30, 1918, with the civil war still raging and the Bolshevik hold on power precarious, Lenin was shot. He survived – but only just.

Lenin's would-be assassin was 28-year-old Socialist Revolutionary, Fanny Kaplan. Interrogated by the Cheka, Kaplan said, "Today I shot at Lenin. I did it on my own. I will not say from whom I obtained my revolver. I will give no details. I had resolved to kill Lenin long ago. I consider him a traitor to the Revolution".

The Cheka, desperate to know who Kaplan was working for, got nothing out of her. So, at 4 am on September 3, Fanny Kaplan was escorted into a garage and executed with a single bullet to the back of her head. Her corpse was bundled into a barrel and set alight. Lenin's near death at the hands of a deranged woman suited the Bolsheviks at a time when their survival looked far from certain. Lenin profited from a surge of sympathy that served both him and his party well.

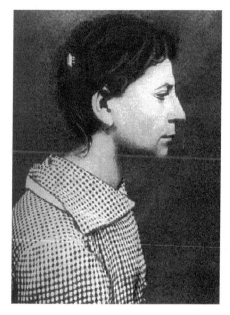

Fanny Kaplan, 1918.

Red Terror

The day following Kaplan's execution, the Bolsheviks launched their campaign of "Red Terror". Felix "Iron" Dzerzhinsky, the first head of the Cheka, openly declared, "We stand for organized terror – this should be frankly admitted. Terror is an absolute necessity during times of revolution".

On November 11, 1918, the Great War came to an end with the signing of the Western Front armistice. One of the conditions forced upon defeated Germany was the complete annulment of the Treaty of Brest-Litovsk. The Treaty of Brest-Litovsk may have given Poland, Finland and the Baltic States their independence, but the annulment of the treaty meant they had to fight the Reds in order to maintain it. Bitter fighting ensued, including the Russo-Polish War and the Finnish Civil War. By the end of the Russian Civil War, they had all gained their independence but not so Ukraine and Belorussia, both of whom fell under Russian control.

Following the armistice, the Western Allies withdrew much of their troops from Russia. With Trotsky in charge, the Reds slowly gained the upper hand. The Whites' inherent weakness was their lack of cohesion and unity. Pockets of fighting continued in Russia up to June 1923, but from the end of 1919, the result was never truly in doubt – the Reds had won a brutal, horrifying war that had claimed the lives of millions and devastated the country.

War Communism remained deeply unpopular resulting in numerous revolts across the country. The ravages of the civil war, Lenin's policy of grain requisitioning and a severe drought in 1921 caused a famine, especially in the Urals, resulting in the deaths of some six million people.

In February 1921, in an echo of the "Bloody Sunday" demonstrations of 1905, people came out on the streets of

Petrograd, venting their anger against Lenin's one-party government and his War Communism policy. Lenin's troops shot them down. Nothing much had changed from tsarist times – except it was worse.

It was the Kronstadt Uprising of March 1921 that shocked Lenin. The Kronstadt naval garrison, about 20 miles from Petrograd, was considered one of the Bolshevik's most loyal supporters. But by February, even they had had enough. They demanded a return to multi-party, soviet power, as opposed to one-party Bolshevik power. They demanded a return of press freedom and freedom of speech, and demanded the abolition of Lenin's feared Cheka.

Lenin may have been shocked by the mutiny of his supposedly most loyal followers but it didn't stop him from brutally suppressing the revolt. Kronstadt was separated from the mainland by a strip of water but in March that water is frozen over. Led by Trotsky, Red Army troops crossed the ice and despite initial losses brought the uprising to a speedy and bloody end. Scores of mutineers were executed.

Just at the point the Kronstadt Uprising was breaking out in March 1921, the communist party opened their tenth party congress in Moscow, the first since the end of the Civil War. The party was at a watershed: news of the uprising came through, there were peasant uprisings elsewhere, War

Communism was proving a catastrophe, and party members, forming into offshoot groups, had begun arguing amongst themselves. Lenin needed to prove himself. His first step was to issue a decree entitled "On Party Unity", which strictly forbade all disagreement and offshoots. Any party member breaking the decree would be expelled and punished. Lenin had made it clear – he would not tolerate any debate.

Next, Lenin announced the abandonment of War Communism, to be replaced by a "New Economic Policy". NEP permitted a limited return to capitalist trade – peasants were now allowed to sell their produce on the open market. Grain requisition was halted which encouraged the peasant to grow more. Many in the party hated it – they felt their leader was selling communism out to capitalism. But it was for Lenin "one step backwards in order to take two steps forward".

Over the coming months, NEP proved to be, by and large, a great success. As with any form of capitalism – there were those who did well and those who did not. Those who prospered earned the nickname "NEPmen" from those who did not.

Man of Steel

During late March / early April 1922, the party held its

eleventh congress. It was here that the role of "general secretary" was first introduced, a role that was indeed secretarial to begin with, involving administrative work. The first person to hold the post was one Joseph Vissarionovich Dzhugashvili from Georgia. The post of general secretary soon became the term associated with the party leader and head of government.

Dzhugashvili had played an important if minor role during the October Revolution of 1917. He'd first met Lenin back in January 1906 at a party conference in Finland. Lenin was impressed with Dzhugashvili, calling him the "wonderful Georgian". Dzhugashvili's name was too Georgian and, for his Russian colleagues, too difficult to pronounce, hence he began calling himself Stalin, "man of steel".

Following the "July Days" demonstration, Stalin had helped Lenin escape first to the forests outside Petrograd, then to Finland, advising Lenin to shave off his trademark beard. During the Russian Civil War, Stalin successfully and brutally defended the city of Tsaritsyn (renamed Stalingrad in 1925, and now called Volgograd).

The month following Stalin's appointment as general secretary, Lenin suffered his first stroke which deprived him of speech and hampered his movement. After six months of rest, he returned to work, but on a lighter schedule.

Joseph Stalin, 1918.

In December 1922, while recuperating, Lenin wrote his "Testament", in which he proposed changes to the structure of the party's Central Committee. Lenin began his Testament with his concerns over the open hatred between Trotsky and Stalin.

Stalin visits Lenin during Lenin's recuperation, 1922.

He praised and criticized various members of the committee, including Trotsky. His most damning view however was reserved for Joseph Stalin. Lenin was regretting his haste in promoting Stalin to the post of general secretary. He described Stalin as having "unlimited authority concentrated in his hands ... I am not sure whether he will always be capable of using that authority with sufficient caution". He called Stalin "rude" and suggested that his comrades *"think about a way of removing Stalin from that post and appointing another man in his stead who in all other respects differs from*

Comrade Stalin in having only one advantage, namely, that of being more tolerant, more loyal, more polite, and more considerate to the comrades, less capricious, etc.".

Lenin's wife, Nadezhda Krupskaya, kept her husband's Testament secret in the hope that he would recover. He never did.

In the same month as issuing his testament, December 1922, Lenin's government passed the Treaty on the Creation of the USSR, thereby officially establishing the Union of Soviet Socialist Republics.

The Death of Lenin

Having suffered three strokes (not helped by the bullet wounds suffered in 1918 at the hands of Fanny Kaplan) Vladimir Lenin, aged 53, died on January 21, 1924.

Wanting to be seen as Lenin's natural successor, Stalin took charge of the funeral arrangements, assuming the roles of lead pallbearer and chief mourner. Trotsky, his rival for power, missed Lenin's funeral entirely having been given the wrong date by the scheming Stalin.

A million mourners paid their respects as Lenin lay in state for four days in Moscow's House of Unions. Three days after his death, Petrograd was renamed Leningrad. Scientists removed Lenin's brain and kept it in formaldehyde for two years before slicing it into 30,963 wafer-thin slices in order to work out how the brain of a genius worked. Lenin's corpse was embalmed and placed in a wooden mausoleum in Moscow's Red Square. In October 1930, Lenin was placed in the marble and granite mausoleum that for 60 years became the spiritual home of communism and where it still remains to this day.

Lenin's funeral, January 23, 1924.

Nadezhda Krupskaya, Lenin's widow, insisted that her husband's Testament be read out at the party's Thirteenth Party Congress, due in May 1924. Stalin had managed to form a ruling threesome with Kamenev and Zinoviev, primarily to keep Trotsky from assuming power. Lenin's Testament had criticized all three, especially Stalin, and they could not afford such a critical document to be made public. Krupskaya protested but only carefully chosen sections were read out at the congress. Hence, Lenin's questions over Stalin's suitability were suppressed and were never permitted to be mentioned again. Stalin had survived.

The era of Stalin was about to begin. It was to last until his death almost thirty years later

Trotsky was increasingly marginalised by the party to the point in January 1925 he was relieved of his post. Zinoviev and Kamenev, two-thirds of the ruling trio, themselves fell out with Stalin and joined forces with Trotsky. In October 1927, Trotsky was expelled from the Central Committee and the following month from the Communist Party altogether.

In January 1928, Trotsky was exiled to Kazakhstan and finally banished from the Soviet Union in February 1929. Eventually, Trotsky settled in Mexico. Meanwhile, Moscow hosted the first of the infamous Show Trials in which old Bolsheviks, such as Lev Kamenev and Grigory Zinoviev, confessed to various anti-state crimes and having acted under the instructions of Trotsky. All were sentenced to death, including Trotsky who was found guilty in his absence. Kamenev and Zinoviev were both executed in August 1936.

On August 20, 1940, Trotsky was attacked at home by an undercover Soviet agent, Ramón Mercader. Fatally wounded by a head wound caused by an ice pick, Leon Trotsky died in hospital the following day.

The USSR lasted from its formal establishment in December 1922 to its dissolution on December 25, 1991. Joseph Stalin remained general secretary until his death on March 5, 1953. He was succeeded after a few months of hiatus by Nikita Khrushchev. Khrushchev was ousted from power in 1964 to be replaced by Leonid Brezhnev, who remained in office until his death in November 1982. He was succeeded by Yuri Andropov, who died in office in February 1984, and then Konstantin Chernenko, who died in office in March 1985. Chernenko, in turn, was succeeded by the relative youngster, 54-year-old Mikhail Gorbachev. And it was during Gorbachev's era that the ruling communist power collapsed and the Soviet Union was dissolved.

After seven decades, Russia's great experiment with communism had come to an end.

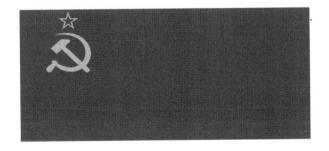

Russian Revolution Timeline

(Note: all dates are recorded in the New Style, introduced after the October Revolution)

1861

March 3   Tsar Alexander II issues his edict on the emancipation of the serfs.

1881

March 13   Assassination of Tsar Alexander II, succeeded by his son, Alexander III.

1887

May 20   Execution of Aleksandr Ulyanov, Vladimir Lenin's brother, for the attempted assassination of Tsar Alexander III.

1894

November 1   Death of Tsar Alexander III, succeeded by his son, Nicholas II.

1903

November 17   Second Congress of the Russian Social Democratic Party (RSDP), during which the party splits into factions: Menshevik and Bolshevik.

1904

February 8   Start of the Russo-Japanese War with Japan's attack on Russian ships based at Port Arthur in Manchuria.

1905

January 22   "Bloody Sunday" massacre on the streets of St Petersburg.

May 27-28   Russo-Japanese War: defeat of the Russian navy in the Tsushima Strait.

June 27   Mutiny on the Battleship Potemkin.

September 5   The end of the Russo-Japanese War.

October   Russia seized by national strikes.

October 30   Tsar Nicholas II issues his "October Manifesto".

Oct-Dec   Workers' councils, or "soviets", spring up in Russian cities.

1906

May   The tsar re-asserts his autocratic rule.

July 21   First Duma dissolved. Pyotr Stolypin

appointed prime minister.

1911

September 14   Pyotr Stolypin assassinated. He dies four
days later.

1914

June 28   Archduke Franz Ferdinand of Austria-
Hungary assassinated in Sarajevo.

August 1   First World War: Germany declares war on
Russia.

1916

December 30   Murder of Georgi Rasputin.

1917

March 8-12   The "February" Revolution begins with
strikes and demonstrations in Petrograd
against the tsar and demands to end Russia's
participation in the war. Formation of the
Petrograd soviet. Demonstrations soon
spread to other cities.

March 15   Nicholas II forced to abdicate. Formation
of the Provisional Government headed by

Prince Georgy Lvov. Country run by a "Dual Power" – the Provisional Government and the soviets.

April 16   Lenin returns to Russia, arriving in Petrograd from Germany.

April 17   Lenin issues his "April Thesis".

June 29   First World War: Alexander Kerensky, the Provisional Government's Minister for War, launches the "Kerensky Offensive".

July 16-20   The "July Days" demonstrations against the Provisional Government.

 Lenin flees Petrograd, eventually arriving in Finland.

July 21   Prince Lvov resigns as head of the Provisional Government and is replaced by Alexander Kerensky.

August 31   Bolsheviks became the majority party within the Petrograd Soviet.

Sept 8-12   The "Kornilov Affair", Kerensky's failed attempt to use Lavr Kornilov to subdue the Petrograd soviet.

October 23   Lenin returns to Petrograd urging immediate revolution.

November 7   The "October" Revolution takes place in

Petrograd and soon spreads. The
Provisional Government is dissolved.
Second All-Russian Congress of Soviets is
convened.

November 8 Second All-Russian Congress of Soviets
issues decrees on land and peace, and
establishes its first government and cabinet,
with Lenin its head.

November Start of the Russian Civil War.

November 25 National elections to the Constituent
Assembly.

December 16 First World War: Russia signs armistice with
Germany and its allies.

December 20 The "All-Russian Extraordinary
Commission for Combating Counter-
Revolution and Sabotage", better known as
the "Cheka", is established.

1918

January 18 Constituent Assembly meets for the sole
time in Petrograd.

January 19 Lenin dissolves the Constituent Assembly.

March 3 The Treaty of Brest-Litovsk, formally
ending Russia's involvement in the First

	World War, is signed with Germany.
March 8	The Bolshevik party officially changes its name to the Russian Communist Party.
March 12	Lenin moves the seat of the government and the Russian capital from Petrograd to Moscow
June	Lenin introduces "War Communism".
July 17	Nicholas II and family are murdered.
August 30	Lenin shot and wounded by would-be assassin, Fanny Kaplan.
September 3	Policy of "Red Terror" announced.
November 11	End of the First World War.
November 13	Treaty of Brest-Litovsk is annulled.

1919

February	Start of the Russian-Polish War.

1920

October 18	Armistice signed, ending Russian-Polish War.

1921

March 7-17	The Kronstadt Uprising.
March 8-16	Tenth Party Congress bans factions within

the Russian Communist Party.

March 21   Lenin officially ends policy of War Communism and introduces instead his "New Economic Policy", or NEP.

1922

April   Joseph Stalin appointed General Secretary of the Communist Party's Central Committee.

May   Lenin suffers his first stroke.

December   Lenin writes his "Testament".

December 30   Formation of the Union of Soviet Socialist Republics.

1924

January 21   Lenin dies aged 53.

January 24   Petrograd renamed Leningrad.

Images

All the images used in this book are, as far as the publisher can ascertain, in the public domain. If they have mistakenly used an image that is not in the public domain, please let them know at felix@historyinanhour.com and they shall remove / replace the offending item.

The Clever Teens series available as paperback and ebook:

The Clever Teens' Guide to World War One

The Clever Teens' Guide to the Russian Revolution

The Clever Teens' Guide to Nazi Germany

The Clever Teens' Guide to World War Two

The Clever Teens' Guide to the Cold War

The Clever Teens' Guide Bumper Edition: Five Books in One (ebook only)

The Clever Teens Tales From World War One

The Clever Teens Tales From World War Two

Visit **https://rupertcolley.com/category/soviet-union-russia/** for 13 articles expanding on topics covered here.